NORMAL
SEX

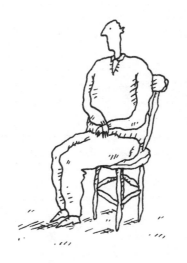

For my Mum and Dad
and Nicola

Many thanks to: Ros Badger, Jonathan Boatfield,
Liz Calder, Maryclare Foa, Malcolm Garrett,
Kasper de Graaf, Richard Ingrams, Ben Murphy,
Anita Plank & Kjartan Poskitt

Special thanks to: George Mole (pages 119 - 127),
Pete Bishop (50 & 87), Joe Ewart (35).

Some of these drawings previously appeared
in: Punch, Tatler, Company, Harpers & Queen,
Esquire, The Guardian, The Observer, Blueprint,
Time Out, Skin Two, The Oldie & Blitz.

First Harper Collins Edition Published in 1994.

Library of Congress Cataloging in Publication Data
ISBN 0-06-251153-x

94 95 96 97 98 HAD 10 9 8 7 6 5 4 3 2 1

This edition is printed on acid-free paper that meets the
American National Standards Institute 239.48 standard.

NORMAL SEX

Steven Appleby

HarperSanFrancisco
A Division of HarperCollins*Publishers*

The author and a friend conduct
some essential research.

CONTENTS...

Part One
UNDERSTANDING THE OPPOSITE SEX
Relationships, Love, Marriage & Guilt

Part Two
PRACTICAL THINGS TO WORRY ABOUT
Sex, Contraception & Improving Your
Appearance

Part Three
IMPRACTICAL THINGS TO WORRY ABOUT
Perversions & Deviations, The Sex Life of
Machines & Taboos

Part Four
THE JOY OF BEING SINGLE
Living on your Own, Sex With Yourself

APPENDICES
Appendix I – Men the Truth
Appendix II – A side effect
Appendix III – Courtship & Reproduction On Other
                Planets
Appendix IV – Answers to Infertility

Part One

UNDERSTANDING
THE OPPOSITE SEX

FIRST THINGS FIRST

fig 1 – The basic equipment:

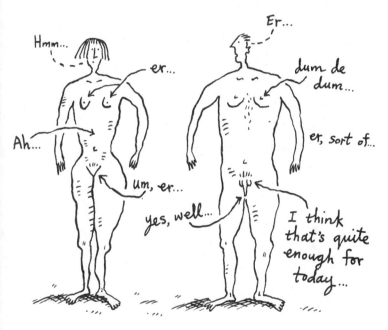

A WOMAN   A MAN

Usually one of these is attracted to the other, and vice versa.

Darling...

SIGH...

Some individuals are attracted only to themselves.

Other confused people suspect that they may belong to an as yet undiscovered sex.

I don't know if I'm heterosexual, gay, or...

maybe I'm TRI-SEXUAL!

Of course creepy-crawlies have sexual worries too. Worms have trouble deciding which end is which...

Is this my head?

or this?

which end do I put the condom on?

And amoeba agonise over when to divide.

Is my relationship with myself stable enough for children?

8

Even celestial opposites have doubts about their relationships. Day can't work Night out at all.

He's so gloomy!

But the main thing is not to lose heart. Somewhere there will be a person or object compatible with you no matter how unlikeable, repulsive and unbearable you are.

Will you go out with me?

I'd rather die.

SOME DIFFERENT KINDS OF RELATIONSHIPS:

2 people:

2 people and a friend:

move over!

2 people of the same sex:

2 people of the same sex and a friend:

How do you do...

1 real person and an inflatable person:

wheeze...

Mr Whipple and Fido:

Good boy.

Ms Brown and Dibble:

An Optimist:

A pessimist:

Eleven people of assorted sexes:

Mr and Mrs Dobbs and a visitor from outer space:

2 people who used to get on:

the WHEEL of POSSIBLE PARTNERS...

A MARRIED MAN
But you're married!
Yes — to you!

A LIFE OF CELIBACY
Purr... Purr... Purr... Purr...

TOTAL IGNORANCE
The opposite what?

Um...

KINKY...
I like to dress up as a rabbit.
oh dear...
HOP...

PLATONIC
We can talk about sex without any complications — or any sex.

12

13

HOW A RELATIONSHIP WORKS –

THE SCIENTIFIC ANALYSIS.

i – Thoughts...

Deceitful little weasel

ii – ... are translated into air movement by the lungs, lips and tongue.

LIPS

AIR

TONGUE

LUNGS

iii – This air motion is then turned back into words by the recipient's ear:

I HATE YOU!!

Pardon?

when things go wrong
A CAUTIONARY TALE...

Despite all claims to the contrary, the aim in any relationship is for one party to gain the upper hand over the other.

This approach has resulted in many years during which human beings have dominated their environment — but perhaps the balance is about to shift...

An early sign of changes in the status quo:

? darling?

Not tonight — I have a headache.

Soon other components of the body begin questioning their identities...

hello? what?

who's there? ho ho ho ho...

Where? ssssh!

hup hup hup... hang on a minute!

Next, inanimate objects prepare to renegotiate their positions...

? It's good to take the weight off my feet!

oof!!

LOVE

Love is a kind of insanity and people suffering from it should be treated cautiously as they won't listen to a word you say while expecting you to be fascinated by all sorts of far-fetched and implausible stories about someone you probably haven't met and don't want to. Pouring a bucket of water over them is not much use as the madness is too deeply ingrained, but it may make you feel better.

I love Jesus!

Hallelujah!!

Weirdo

PORTENTS of LOVE:

We all look for help when making a decision – particularly regarding our relationships. Some people read tea leaves, others the stars.

you'll have 60 sons and a daughter...

This lady specialises in interpreting the subtle nuances of a door opening.

While this man bases his entire life on random cloud configurations.

SHE HATES YOU!

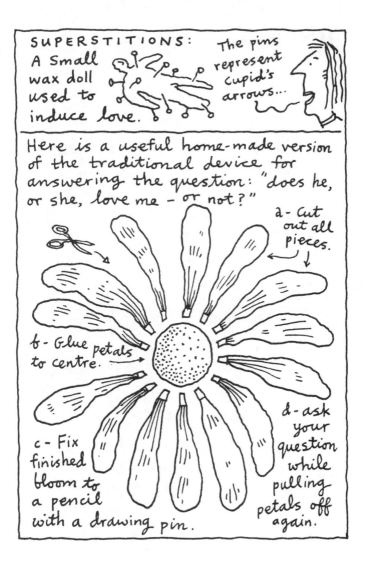

SUPERSTITIONS: A small wax doll used to induce love.

The pins represent cupid's arrows...

Here is a useful home-made version of the traditional device for answering the question: "does he, or she, love me — or not?"

a - Cut out all pieces.

b - Glue petals to centre.

c - Fix finished bloom to a pencil with a drawing pin.

d - ask your question while pulling petals off again.

UNREQUITED LOVE.

Love smites all things – but in this case
is never consummated due to a lack
of communication.

2.

Here both parties remain unfulfilled due to
the one-sided nature of their conversation.

3.

In this example communication seems to be taking place but without reaching a happy conclusion.

4. MEANWHILE ON A GRANDER SCALE:

Could millennia of missed opportunities and awkward silences at last be over?

THINGS TO SAY WHEN YOU'RE IN LOVE:

I love you.
You're wonderful.
Yes you really are.
You're marvellous.
I can't believe this
 is happening.
I really do love you.
You're incredible...

PRACTICAL THINGS TO SAY:

Oh, for goodness sake!
Pull yourself together.
Don't be stupid.
Shut up.

THINGS TO THINK:

How long will it last?
Am I deluding myself?
Is she deluding herself?
Does she love me as
 much as I love her?
I can't stop thinking
 about her!
I can't
 sleep.
Aargh!!

PRACTICAL THING TO THINK:

Dum de dum de
 dum dum hum...

MODERN MARRIAGE

GUILT

There's really nothing quite like sex for providing food for guilt of every sort... so it's pointless to feel guilty — unless you get some kind of pleasure out of it.

You disgusting, deceitful, slimeball of a worm-like abhorrent speck!!

You should be ashamed of yourself!

Oh, I am!

Punish me!

A Catholic gets out of the wrong side
of the wrong bed.

i – HONEST GUILT

Please forgive me...

please...

ii – DECEITFUL GUILT

I'm not going to admit anything at all!

iii – OVER-REACTING GUILT

I'm going to kill myself and the dog!

Oh no! Not the dog!

iv – DELICIOUS GUILT

my tenth cream horn!

who cares!

With every sexual lie he tells,
The adult Pinocchio's erection swells.

Part Two

PRACTICAL THINGS TO WORRY ABOUT

Squeak
Squeak
squeak...

glug!

PRACTICALITIES

Many people have trouble coping with the reality of sex.
For example, this man keeps it in a little compartment as far away from the rest of his life as possible.

Whatever you do don't go in there!

Mr Jimjams allows it to fester, forgotten for years on end, in a damp and unhealthy little corner.

Ugh! Rather hot and squidgy!

Mrs Beelzebub, a lady with firm convictions, pretends that sex doesn't exist so successfully that it doesn't.

I beg your pardon young whatever-you-are!

Wash your mouth out!

Hello miss.

Mr P. - who has rather unusual and amusing needs - tries his hardest to be exactly the same as everyone else.

June F. desperately yearns for a sexual partner even though she knows from past experience that she prefers being out in the garden with a trowel and some bedding plants.

30

Teenagers make a mountain out of sex, which they attempt to climb without proper training or safety equipment. Mr Whipple, 67, hasn't even heard of sex. For the past 37 years he has been constructing a full-size replica of the Grand Canyon entirely from matches which eventually he will try to jump on a Harley Davidson made from string.

Help!

Aagh!

Yow!

Damned kids!

put put put...

Mr Whipple narrowly misses some falling teenagers.

THE SENSITIVE BITS

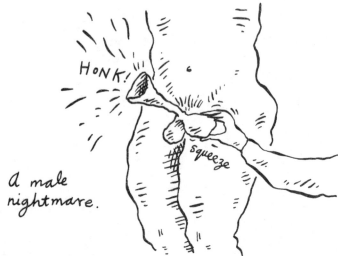

a male
nightmare.

GROIN HORNS - an evolutionary cul-de-sac
in the testicle protection
department:

Making a mountain out of a molehill...

A USEFUL EASTERN SEXUAL TECHNIQUE:

The Indian Penis Trick.

SEX EDUCATION

Inventing new sexual positions:

a - The Granny Knot.

b - The Helicopter.

c - The Steam Train.

d - The Stepladder.

e - The Astronaut.

Roger?

I'm up here, over.

Roger, roger.

f - On the telephone.

Oooh yes...
ooh yes
yes...

g - The In-the-other-room.

Darling? Darling?

h - Position 96 (in which you both get to go to sleep).

35

AN EXTRACT FROM 'THE BORING SEX GUIDE' (Volume 4)

AN EXTRACT FROM 'THE ENCYCLOPAEDIA OF SEXUAL POSITIONS & DEVIATIONS': MONOGAMY.

SEXUAL TECHNIQUE - some erogenous zones and some erroneous zones.

A few of the 600 or so penis erogenous zones:

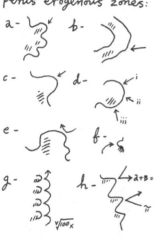

a-
b-
c-
d- i ii iii
e-
f-
g- $\sqrt[x]{100}x$
h- $a+b=$

FOOT FUN!
Specific parts of the foot correspond to parts of the body - see chart below.

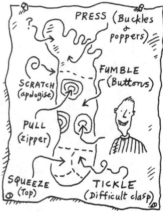

PRESS (Buckles & poppers)

FUMBLE (Buttons)

SCRATCH (apologise)

PULL (zipper)

SQUEEZE (Top)

TICKLE (Difficult clasp)

A device for arousing some internal erogenous zones:

Pants down!

er...

Manipulating the little-known tongue erogenous zones:

Mnnng...

AN ORGY

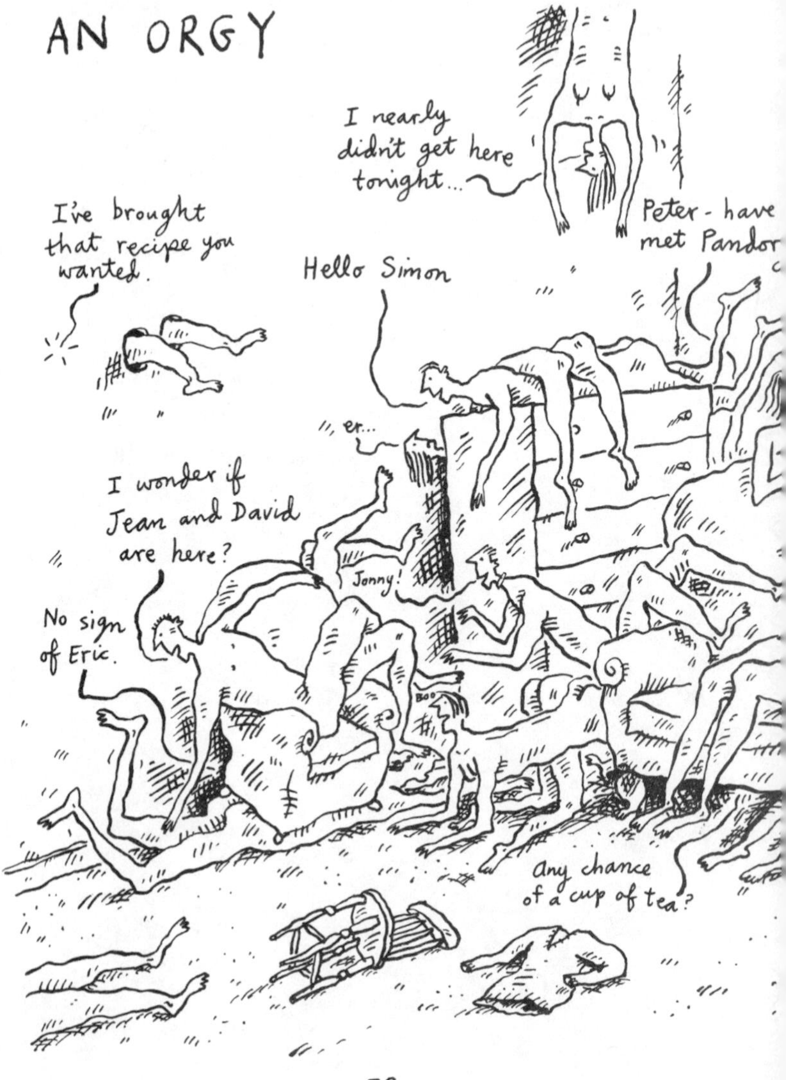

I nearly didn't get here tonight...
I've brought that recipe you wanted.
Hello Simon
Peter - have met Pandor
er...
I wonder if Jean and David are here?
Jonny!
No sign of Eric.
Boo
Any chance of a cup of tea?

39

A GUIDE TO ORGASMS:

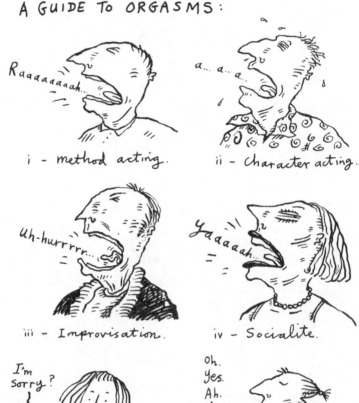

Raaaaaaaaah...

i - method acting.

a... a.. a...

ii - character acting.

Uh-hurrrrr...

iii - Improvisation.

Yaaaaah...

iv - Socialite.

I'm sorry?

Have you finished?

I wasn't paying attention...

v - Long-term partner.

Oh. Yes. Ah.

Thank you.

vi - Polite.

HOME SEX THERAPIST:

For those who can't climax, here is a foolproof way to reach orgasm. The special chart below (Patent Applied For But Laughed at) will, when read from start (point a) to finish (point z) result in a fully satisfactory experience induced by eye muscle movement alone. Attractively designed to look good in a frame by the bed for emergency use.

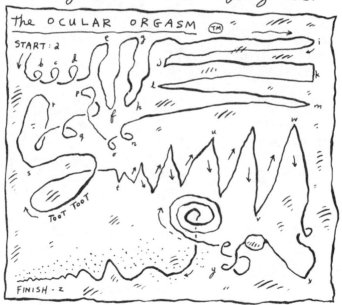

If YOUR sex life is boring, why not add a little spice with one of these non-toxic SEX TOYS...

A vibrating Something-or-other. Available in flesh colour (dead) or purple. Batteries not included.

A superb whatsit - and good value at the moment - HURRY while stocks last! Blue only.

A large washable thingy - One size only.

A set of 3 edible what-do-you-call-its. Just what the doctor would order if he knew!

A realistic doo-dah - in presentation case. Instructions enclosed.

SPECIAL OFFER

Glow-in-the-dark 'His 'n' Hers' ™ underwear! Putting out the lights won't extinguish the passion! Now you can find one another in the dark! Guaranteed...

CONTRACEPTION

A WARNING!

A SENSIBLE PRECAUTION:

ASSORTED CONDOM DESIGNS:

Cute NOVELTY ANIMAL CONDOMS:

a.

b.

c.

THE
'CATAMARAN'
A novelty condom...
Presumably.

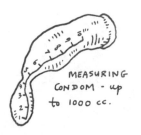

MEASURING
CONDOM - up
to 1000 cc.

AN EDIBLE CONDOM:

available in brown, white
or granary.
 WARNING - On its own
 does not constitute
 a balanced diet -
 must be supplemented
 by beer and snacks.

KNITTED WOOLLEN CONDOM:

If it was good enough for your Grandad, blah blah blah...

A present from Grandma (who had fifteen children).

TOTAL PROTECTION:

mmmmng?*

The complete body condom.

*Shall we go to bed darling?

THE 'OPTIMIST'

FINALLY — A special condom approved by the Pope for Roman Catholics:

the HOLY Condom. praise him!

Learning how to put on a condom using various vegetables and household items:

A TURNIP.

A LETTUCE.

A TELEPHONE.

A GRAPE.

We'll need two.

A CAR.

AN UNFORTUNATE MIX-UP AT THE RUBBER PRODUCTS FACTORY.

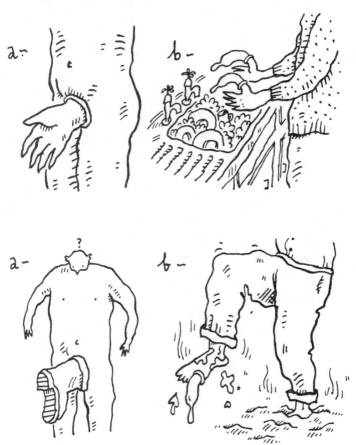

ALTERNATIVES to the CONDOM

fig a –

fig b – Reading a good book.

fig c – A double chastity belt.

A NEW KIND OF BIRTH CONTROL

Homing sperm.

SAFE SEX

Safe Sex using imagination alone to achieve satisfaction:

MODERN NEUROSIS:

Pre-Sex sterilisation.

a Digression...

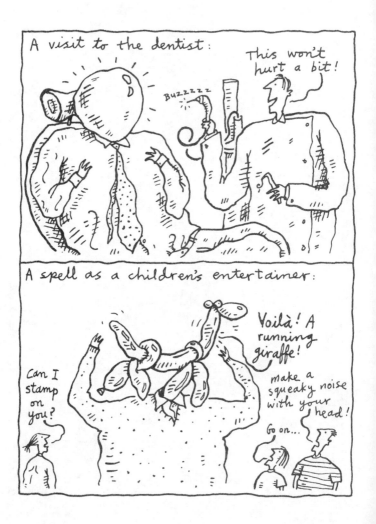

52

An embarrassing adhesive moment caused by a build-up of static electricity:
I'm terribly sorry - are you wearing nylon?

Darling...
mmmm?..
True Love - Mr Balloon meets his future wife during a brief career as a Christmas decoration.

IMPROVE YOUR APPEARANCE

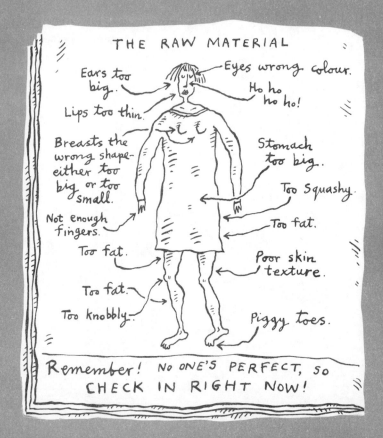

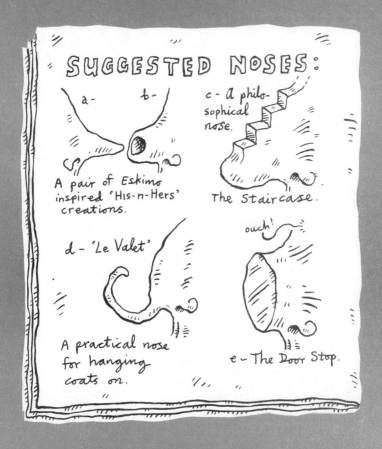

SUGGESTED NOSES:

a-   b-

c - A philo-
sophical
nose.

A pair of Eskimo
inspired 'His-n-Hers'
creations.

The Staircase.

d - 'Le Valet'

ouch!

A practical nose
for hanging
coats on.

e - The Door Stop.

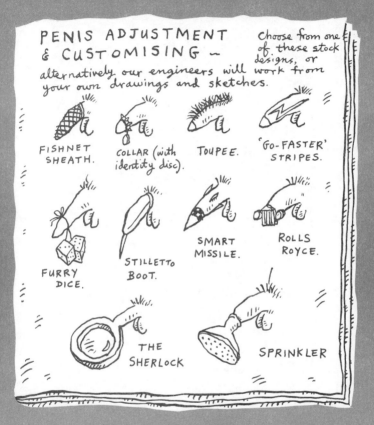

PENIS ADJUSTMENT & CUSTOMISING — Choose from one of these stock designs, or alternatively our engineers will work from your own drawings and sketches.

FISHNET SHEATH.

COLLAR (with identity disc).

TOUPEE.

'GO-FASTER' STRIPES.

FURRY DICE.

STILLETTO BOOT.

SMART MISSILE.

ROLLS ROYCE.

THE SHERLOCK

SPRINKLER

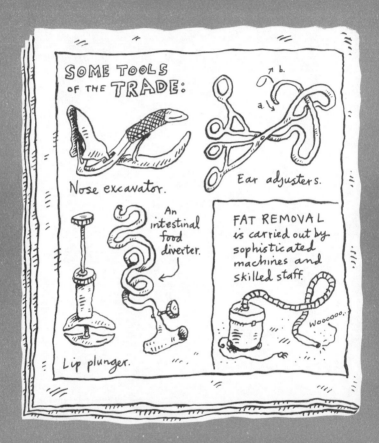

62

WHAT SATISFIED CUSTOMERS HAVE SAID:

Thank you, 'Bob's'

Thank you, 'Bob's'

Thank you, 'Bob's'

Why not apply for Bob's credit card and pay for your restorative surgery at inflated interest rates over a vague and not clearly specified length of time?

Bob's FRANCHISE

A.N. OTHER SUCKER

After your course in plastic surgery a healthy-looking tan is just the thing — but follow these tips to avoid premature aging and skin cancer!

TANNING GUIDE:
a useful chart.

1989:

Before →

after →

1999:

Before →

After →

tanning bag:
(baste frequently)

A SPECIAL OUTFIT FOR DECORATIVE TANNING:

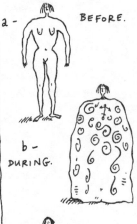

a -   BEFORE.

b - DURING.

c - AFTER.

DECORATIVE SHAVING.

Taking inspiration from the topiary in some of our great ornamental gardens, imaginative clipping can add amusement and interest to an otherwise dull and lack-lustre sex life. Try these at home (or outside if you prefer).

Hair spray and careful tending have resulted in THE QUIFF:

PUBIC PORTRAITS:

i -

ii -

iii -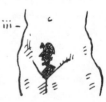

Winston Churchill.   Mother Theresa.   D.H. Lawrence.

POETIC MOMENTS:

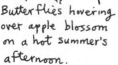

Butterflies hovering over apple blossom on a hot summer's afternoon.

Lion cub lapping at the edge of a pool at dawn.

F1-11 cruising at 15,000 feet stalked by a MIG.

DRESSING UP

Before baring your all, you need to impress with your attire. Carefully chosen clothing can work wonders by concealing the uglier, wobblier parts and highlighting the occasional pleasing bit.

THE EMPEROR'S NEW CLOTHES...

I think I preferred the invisible suit I didn't see earlier...

fabulous...

The invisible suit turns out to be the best of a bad lot.

CLOTHES TO BE SEEN IN IN...

BOOB TUBES -

with magnifying lenses!

A RUBBERIST -

I'm erasing!

SKIN TIGHT -

That IS my skin!

SKIMPY -

Oops - I forgot to put anything on at all!

THONG

THING

THONGY-THING

Three nudists wearing clothes.

TRYING OUT CORSETS:

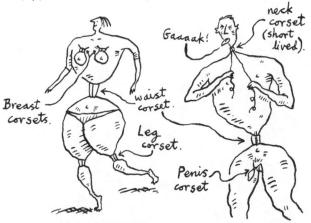

Breast corsets.

waist corset.

Leg corset.

neck corset (short lived).

Gaaaak!

Penis corset

EXPERIMENTING with a porcupine suit:

Big hug!

Seen here concealed beneath street clothes:

Hello vicar.

A TYPICAL SCENE IN THE SUBURBS:

Part Three

IMPRACTICAL THINGS TO WORRY ABOUT

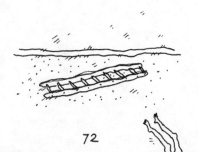

PERVERSIONS & DEVIATIONS

More and more people these days enjoy a good, healthy fetish.

Roger and Gillian X, for example, enjoy drinking cups of tea off each other's bodies — are they abnormal?

A rural man who prefers to remain anonymous, gets pleasure from dressing as a lettuce, being watered, thinned out and re-potted in the greenhouse.

cover me in French dressing!

It's getting a bit dark in here.

Mr. P from Herne Hill likes dressing as a bedside lamp and being turned on.

Reading is an interest which
many people develop, and
David L — dressed as a large
wasp — chews his copy of

The Times
into a paste
and uses
it to
wallpaper
his room.

But some people go too far!
In the interest of public decency
we simply cannot print a
picture of the perverts who
derive some sort of disturbed
pleasure from the wearing of
brightly coloured nylon
sportswear.

A DOUBLE PERVERSION

A man, dressed as a woman, dressed as a man.

HOW DOES IT START?

Here we see that some sexual fetishes grow from experiences rooted in early childhood...

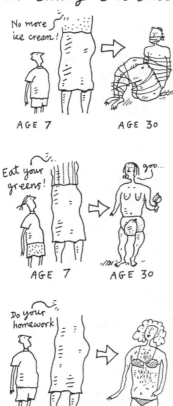

No more ice cream!

AGE 7   AGE 30

Eat your greens!   goo...

AGE 7   AGE 30

Do your homework

AGE 7   AGE 30

THE BUTTOCKHEADS

Caught out by his wife in a minor misdemeanour, Mr Buttockhead indulges in a predictably conventional sexual fantasy.

Spank my face!

THE EFFECT IN LATER LIFE OF BANNING CANING IN SCHOOLS:

You naughty boy!

Write me a letter of apology and 200 lines!

oh yes! yes!

Save on electricity with a 'HOOVERIST' –
the useful side of fetishism.

This top-of-
the-range
model picks
up cat hairs
and shampoos
the
carpet!

Whoooo

Mr Hetherington-Fotherington is a peer of
the realm and rather expensive.

This 'HIS-N-HERS' tongue clamp is essential for the couple who appreciate the exquisite subtlety of being unable to kiss.

Furniture fetishists:

Two Santa Claus fetishists:

A jug (or genie) fetishist:

A CAR FETISHIST POLISHING:

TWO SCRABBLE PLAYERS:

FOOD **AND** FETISHISM:

You've had your cake, Simon - now go make your bed and lie in it!

FOOD & FOOTWEAR: exotic sexual appetites can sometimes be satisfied with shoes made out of pastry, chocolate and fresh cream.

1:

2:

SPLUDGE!

DON'T WORRY
if you've got a
FOOD FETISH

You're not peculiar —
everyone else has one too!

Everyone except
me, of course!

You
perverts!

Ha ha
ha

Don't be embarrassed if you
feel the urge to dress as a
rubber glove and splash about
in a huge sink full of giant
crockery.

It's quite natural to wear a
carrot suit and climb into
an enormous steamer.

You should be
boiled to within an
inch of your life!

Steaming
is the
modern
way!

Gregory likes to pollinate
rhubarb ~ so far with a
sad lack of success.

I must
write to
Gardeners'
Question
Time...

RHUBARB
PATCH

Roger, who has had a sex change to 'IT', now reproduces like a seedless grape.

Um...

How is that, exactly?...

But some people feel compelled to eat only vegetables, which is a bit weird. Try to be tolerant...

Do you get some sort of sick pleasure out of it?

A healthy pleasure, actually. La la la...

COOKING & SEX

Why not try improvising a sauce for the body using ingredients readily to hand in your kitchen. How about a Welsh Rarebit inspired concoction, or a Banana Custard, perhaps? Delicious hot (not <u>TOO</u> hot) or cold (not <u>TOO</u> cold).

ETIQUETTE TIP – Using a knife and fork is considered bad manners.

LESSER-KNOWN FOOD APPRECIATION SOCIETIES:

The donut club.

Stilletto glasses.

A PERVERSE FLY:

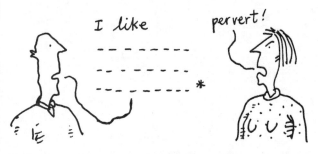

Remember –

PEOPLE ARE UNDERSTANDING AND IT
IS ALWAYS BEST TO BE HONEST AND
OPEN ABOUT YOURSELF...

I like

- - - - -
- - - - -
- - - - - *

pervert!

*Fill in your sexual deviation here.
(Continue on a separate sheet if
necessary.)

the SEX LIFE of MACHINES

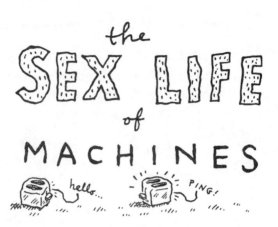

i — One day machines will learn how to reproduce.

Avert your eyes from the kitchen, dears!

Aw...

CLANK CLUNK Rattle CLINK THUD Bump...

But I like watching the cooker and the fridge!

ii ~ Cross breeding will produce some curious hybrids...

These fridge/cookers are a bit disappointing...

My ice-cream is soft!

My pie is raw!

iii ~ ...and some machines will develop curious perversions:

The toaster has started dressing up as a table lamp!

iv ~ When machine relationships turn sour, everyone suffers.

The fridge has moved out of the kitchen for a trial period.

v ~ Finally, an unforeseen consequence:

Dad's with the fridge again.

First it was the T.V. now this!

you make me feel young!

BUZZ...

SEXUAL TABOOS ~ No. 1

Having sex with a dead person.

SEXUAL TABOOS ~ No. 2

ANIMALS.

A horse lover.
(The British are well-known
dog and cat lovers, too.)

Mr Praying Mantis makes
a novel suggestion.

Part Four

THE JOY OF
STAYING SINGLE

LIVING
ON YOUR OWN

Being single is the perfect relationship.
You get to spend twenty-four hours
a day with the person you know and
love best in the world, and of whose
companionship you never tire.

I think I'll do exactly what I
want today, then exactly
what I want again after
that, then...

I love me,
I love me not.
I love me,
I love me not
I ...

A well-adjusted single person
can generally cope with living
alone without falling prey to
obscure religious cults, fluffy-
pet-obsession or hallucinations.
And he or she will soon be able
to bask in the envious glances
of various married friends.

Life begins when you're single.

THE POSITIVE SIDE.

THE NEGATIVE SIDE.

Party time at Mr Unpopular's house.

No. 1 in a series of
USEFUL THINGS to say to
a persistent admirer:

GO AWAY!

SEX WITH YOURSELF

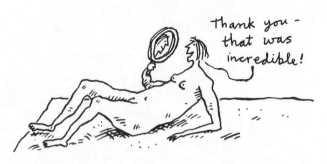

Thank you - that was incredible!

Things to say to yourself in a solo relationship:

Not tonight - I'm washing my hair.

Are you having an affair with a real person?

I'm too tired. Maybe tomorrow...

PROPS & DEVICES for the devotee of solo sex:

A portable motion-powered orifice for day-long comfort.

A USEFUL CHAIR:

hello

A THIRD ARM:

(clockwork mechanism.)

A cup of tea and some chunks of chocolate.

AN INFLATABLE PERSON:

"Wash behind your ears"

Shown here is the Ann Winter's inflatable public school matron. (No orifices whatsoever.)

A CUDDLING MACHINE:

There there...
There there...

CHUG
CHUG
CHUG
CHUG
CHUG...

103

Buying a solo sex machine.

SEX EDUCATION –
Some positions for solo sex:

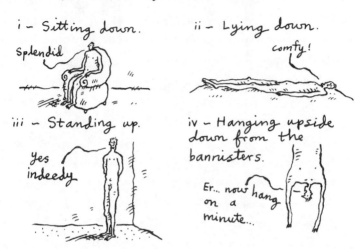

i – Sitting down.

Splendid

ii – Lying down.

comfy!

iii – Standing up.

Yes indeedy

iv – Hanging upside down from the bannisters.

Er... now hang on a minute...

THE SIDE EFFECTS –

Going blind:

Who me?

What rubbish!

Insanity:

I'm going to go and watch soaps on T.V.

AN ORGY:

APPENDICES

They conceal their emotions.

They go bald.

They all like sport.

Size is unimportant.

They have a flair for cooking.

They buy practical clothing
for their loved ones.

MEN 16

They get iller than anyone else.

They are experts with machinery.

They are confident when dealing with women.

They feel like sandpaper.

They make good fathers.

The side effect of sex can be children, who in turn grow up and have more children, and so on. This is something to do with the Meaning of Life.

When I grow up Mum I want to be an inflatable doll.

FEMINIST NIGHTMARE

120

APPENDIX III
Courtship & Reproduction on Other Planets

Let us take an absorbing and educational look into the private affairs and marital arrangements of some typical galactic inhabitants.

WARNING — Some people may find the following material offensive while others, if they have tentacles, more than two heads and strange clusters of sexual organs, could well be led astray by the arousing drawings and erotic text.

uh oh - looks like we're about to have sex.

Buzzzzzzzzz zzz zzz

Plant People of Nimbos having a lie-in.

The universal language of Love.

CHEMICAL ADULTERY - an element arrives home to discover that his gaseous entity has formed a compound with the liquid next door.

A short-sighted Lardat finds he has eloped with a stone.

Spheres making music.

123

GENITALS of the UNIVERSE:

Even the owners of this impressive item don't know exactly what to do with it.

This complex and puzzling apparatus creates problems for the folk of Lego V.

The inhabitants of Glower make fine underarm bowlers thanks to skills developed during their curious method of reproduction.

This rather boring
method of reproduction
is the sad lot
that has fallen
to the rotarians.

↓

It's so small!

Evolution has played
a cruel trick on the
gentle folk of Planet
Percy.

Two residents of
Gelding 4
discover that
they possess
no reproductive
apparatus
whatsoever.

(yawn.)

?

FINALLY – Birth...

The ever-hungry Blutton – a
creature less good-natured than
the stork – is responsible for
delivering the babies on
Planet Mopsy.

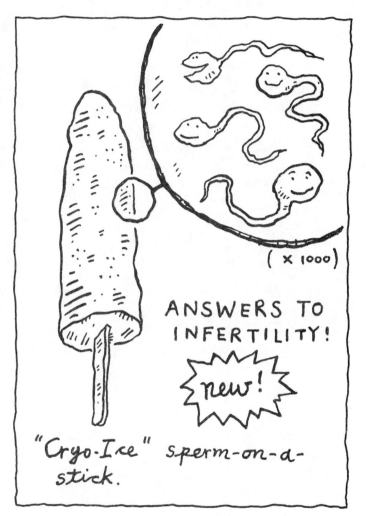

(x 1000)

ANSWERS TO
INFERTILITY!

new!

"Cryo-Ice" sperm-on-a-
stick.